S0-AFB-927

WASHINGTON SCHOOL

208118   551.48 JAC
Lakes

Earthforms

Lakes

by Kay Jackson

Consultant:
John D. Vitek
Assistant Dean of Graduate Studies
Texas A & M University
College Station, Texas

Capstone
press

Mankato, Minnesota

WASHINGTON SCHOOL
122 SOUTH GARFIELD
MUNDELEIN, IL 60060

Bridgestone Books are published by Capstone Press,
151 Good Counsel Drive, P.O. Box 669, Mankato, Minnesota 56002.
www.capstonepress.com

Copyright © 2006 by Capstone Press. All rights reserved.
No part of this publication may be reproduced in whole or in part, or stored in a retrieval
system, or transmitted in any form or by any means, electronic, mechanical, photocopying,
recording, or otherwise, without written permission of the publisher.
For information regarding permission, write to Capstone Press,
151 Good Counsel Drive, P.O. Box 669, Dept. R, Mankato, Minnesota 56002.
Printed in the United States of America

Library of Congress Cataloging-in-Publication Data
Jackson, Kay, 1959–
    Lakes / Kay Jackson.
    p. cm.—(Bridgestone Books. Earthforms)
    Summary: "Describes lakes, including how they form, lake plants and animals, how people and
weather change lakes, Lake Superior, and the Caspian Sea"—Provided by publisher.
    Includes bibliographical references and index.
    ISBN-13: 978-0-7368-5405-4 (hardcover)
    ISBN-10: 0-7368-5405-3 (hardcover)
    1. Lakes—Juvenile literature. I. Title. II. Series.
GB1603.8.J33 2006
551.48'2—dc22   2005015246

Editorial Credits
Becky Viaene, editor; Juliette Peters, set designer; Patrick D. Dentinger, book designer;
    Anne P. McMullen, illustrator; Jo Miller, photo researcher; Scott Thoms, photo editor

Photo Credits
Corbis/Layne Kennedy, 16; Marc Garanger, 18
Eda Rogers, 8
Getty Images Inc./Photodisc Green/Neil Beer, cover
The Image Finders/Jim Baron, 14
Kent Dannen, 4
OneBlueShoe, 1
Seapics.com/Larry Mishkar, 10

1 2 3 4 5 6 11 10 09 08 07 06

Table of Contents

4

What Are Lakes?

A lake is a body of water with land all around. By this definition, it is hard to tell the difference between lakes and **ponds**. The main differences are that lakes are bigger and deeper. Also, more plants grow in shallow ponds than in lakes.

Most lakes are freshwater with little salt. A few are filled with salt water. Great Salt Lake in Utah is saltier than the ocean.

◄ In Colorado, tall mountains of the Sawatch Range surround Mirror Lake.

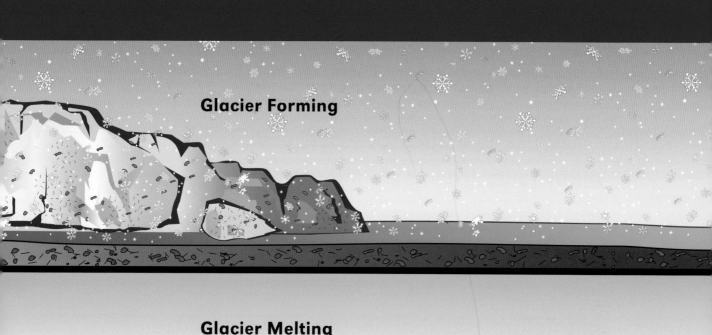

Glacier Forming

Glacier Melting

Ice Blocks

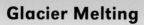

Glacier Melted

Lakes

Lakes

How Do Lakes Form?

Over thousands of years, **glaciers** formed many lakes. As glaciers froze to the ground, they broke off rocks and picked them up. Rock-filled glaciers scraped big holes in the land. As the glaciers melted, giant ice blocks left in holes melted and became lakes.

Some of the world's deepest lakes formed as earth's crust moved apart and created cracks. The cracks slowly filled with water.

People also form lakes by building **dams** across rivers. Dams block the flow of water and form **reservoirs**.

◀ Glaciers melted, scraped holes in the land, and left ice blocks. The ice filled in the holes and formed lakes.

Lake Plants

Most lake plants live in shallow water where sunlight can reach them. Cattails grow along lakes' edges. Their stems grow above the water.

Some plants, like bladderworts, live underwater. Little air sacs on bladderworts help their leaves float near the sunny surface.

Algae float everywhere in lakes. They look like tiny green balls or long thin noodles. Algae-filled lakes may look green.

◄ Tall cattails and bright green moss grow near the edge of this lake.

Lake Animals

Lakes are full of fish. Different types of fish live at different water levels. Minnows hide in mosses along the shore. In deeper water, bass eat diving beetles and other insects. Catfish search for snails and clams on the bottom of the lake.

Other animals spend a lot of time in lakes. Ducks paddle in lake waters. Long-legged herons wade along the shores. Turtles rest on logs. Frogs catch butterflies at edges of lakes.

◄ A largemouth bass swims quickly to catch a meal.

Summer

59 º Fahrenheit (15 º Celsius)

50 º Fahrenheit (10 º Celsius)

Winter

Ice

32 º Fahrenheit (0 º Celsius)

39 º Fahrenheit (4 º Celsius)

Weather Changes Lakes

Weather changes the water temperature of a lake. Warm summer weather heats up the water. The top layer of water gets warm, but the bottom layer stays cold. During winter, the opposite happens. Cold weather may freeze a lake's surface. The lake's bottom does not freeze, because it is warmer than the top.

Weather also changes the size of a lake. During a drought, little rain falls. The lake shrinks when its water **evaporates**. When rain falls again, the lake gets bigger.

◀ Sun and snow can reach the top of the lake. This leaves the bottom colder in summer and warmer in winter.

People Change Lakes

People have found many uses for lakes. They fish in, swim in, and drink water from lakes. Farmers use lakes to water crops. All of these uses can change lakes.

Pollution and overuse harm lakes. Trash and chemical waste are dumped into lakes. Pollution kills animals and plants and makes water unusable. Factories, farmers, and cities may not leave enough water to go around. Lakes can simply dry up when water is overused.

◀ Trash has harmed these ducks' habitat. They will have a hard time finding food in the trash-filled water.

Lake Superior

Lake Superior is one of North America's five Great Lakes and the continent's largest. Lake Superior covers 31,800 square miles (82,362 square kilometers). This lake is almost the same size as the state of South Carolina.

The water temperature in Lake Superior is cold, even in the summer. It stays about 40 degrees Fahrenheit (4.4 degrees Celsius) all year. Diving into deep Lake Superior feels like jumping into ice water.

◄ Even though Lake Superior is the coldest of the Great Lakes, a few people still brave its icy waters to swim.

Caspian Sea

Between Asia and Europe lies the Caspian Sea, the biggest lake on earth. The Caspian is called a sea because it is so large and salty. It covers 143,550 square miles (371,795 square kilometers).

For years, countries have been fighting over the Caspian Sea's resources. Companies from many countries want oil from under its waters. Countries also want fish eggs, called caviar, from the Caspian's beluga sturgeons. These fish produce most of the caviar that people eat.

◄ This small community lies in the middle of the Caspian Sea, where oil wells have been drilled.

WASHINGTON SCHOOL
122 SOUTH GARFIELD
MUNDELEIN, IL 60060

0   100 Miles
0   100 Kilometers

N
W   E
S

CANADA

MINNESOTA

Lake Superior

▼ 1,330 feet
(405 meters)

MICHIGAN

Depth of Lake Superior

0 to 328 feet (0 to 100 meters)

328 to 656 feet (100 to 200 meters)

656 to 984 feet (200 to 300 meters)

Deeper than 984 feet (300 meters)

▼ Deepest point below lake level

UNITED STATES

Lake Michigan

20

WISCONSIN

Lakes on a Map

On colored maps, lakes are blue areas in the middle of land. Some maps even show lake depths. The deepest parts of a lake are shown as dark blue. Light blue shows shallow areas.

Some fishing maps also mark objects hidden underwater. Small squares on the maps show sunken buildings, docks, and boats. These maps help people explore lakes and travel safely on them.

◄ An average depth of about 500 feet (152 meters) makes Lake Superior the deepest of the Great Lakes.

Glossary

algae (AL-jee)—small plants without roots or stems that grow in water or on damp surfaces

dam (DAM)—a barrier built across a river to hold back water

evaporate (e-VAP-uh-rate)—to change from a liquid into a gas

glacier (GLAY-shur)—a moving body of ice

pollution (puh-LOO-shuhn)—harmful materials that damage the air, water, and soil; polluted water can hurt people, plants, and animals.

pond (POND)—an enclosed body of freshwater that is smaller than a lake

reservoir (REZ-ur-vwar)—a natural or artificial holding area for storing large amounts of water; bodies of water behind dams are often called reservoirs.

Read More

Royston, Angela. *Lakes.* My World of Geography. Chicago: Heinemann Library, 2005.

Ylvisaker, Anne. *Lake Superior.* Fact Finders. Land and Water. Mankato, Minn.: Capstone Press, 2004.

Internet Sites

FactHound offers a safe, fun way to find Internet sites related to this book. All of the sites on FactHound have been researched by our staff.

Here's how:
1. Visit *www.facthound*.com
2. Type in this special code **0736854053** for age-appropriate sites. Or enter a search word related to this book for a more general search.
3. Click on the **Fetch It** button.

FactHound will fetch the best sites for you!

Index